BLUR: Friendly Street Poets 29

Amelia Walker began frequenting spoken word
nights when she was sixteen, the same year
she had her first poem published in 'Sidewalk'.
Since then she has performed at many events
and festivals in Adelaide and interstate; her
poetry has been published in various magazines
and journals in Australia and overseas. In 2002
she was the recipient of the Independent Arts
Foundation Scholarship for Literature, which
enabled her to publish her first poetry collection,
Fat Streets & Lots of Squares.

Shen was born in Malaysia and has now lived in
Adelaide for 20 years. He has been published in
many Australian and literary magazines over the
last ten years, and his first collection of poetry,
City of my skin, was published in 2001. He has
long fantasised about extending his poetic
license to his biography, but in the meanwhile,
may just have to settle on also being a GP in
Adelaide's south.

BLUR

Friendly Street Poets 29

Edited by Amelia Walker and Shen

Friendly Street Poets in association with Wakefield Press

Friendly Street Poets Incorporated
in association with
Wakefield Press
1 The Parade West
Kent Town
South Australia 5067

www.friendlystreetpoets.org.au
www.wakefieldpress.com.au

First published 2005

Cover photographs by Amelia Walker
Designed and typeset by Clinton Ellicott, Wakefield Press
Printed and bound by Hyde Park Press

National Library of Australia
Cataloguing-in-publication entry

Blur.

ISBN 1 86254 671 1.

1. Australian poetry – 21st century. I. Walker, Amelia.
II. Shen, 1972–   . III. Friendly Street Poets. (Series:
Friendly Street Poets (Series); 29).

A821.408

Friendly Street is supported by the
South Australian Government through
Arts South Australia.

Wakefield Press thanks Fox Creek Wines
and Arts South Australia for their support.

Contents

Acknowledgements

Poems from this collection have been previously published in the following publications:

ArtState
Blue Dog
Canberra Times
Green Room (Piping Shrike anthology)
Griffith REVIEW
Papertiger (New World Poetry)
Sidewalk

Preface

The first time I picked up *The Box*, my entire body tingled with a mixture of exhilaration and fear. I speak, of course, of the Friendly Street *Box*, with its holographic blue contact peeling at the corners, revealing hints of many past lifecycles and reinventions. I don't know how old it is, though the dreamer in me likes to hope there has only ever been and ever will be one *Box*. Sometimes, when nobody is looking, I open the lid of it just a crack and wedge my nose into that dark space. I imagine I am breathing the ghosts of old poems; published and unpublished; words of hope and despair; love and love lost; war and rebellion; wild manifestoes; tearful sojourns; and of course, cask wine, tannic as the sweat of sixty bodies crammed into the top floor of the Box Factory on a February evening.

Friendly Street has been running longer than I have been alive. Though mostly I use this fact to niggle the insecurities of Friendly Street's original members (sorry, Graham Rowlands!) it is a thought which also fills me with awe. Though *The Box* has floated from desk to car to the kitchen table and even made its way into the laundry on a few occasions over the past year, I still feel a hint of that tingle every time I pick it up. It is a relay baton; a torch of words passed on defiantly for many years now, which shall yet be passed on, and on, and on, as the mad clan that is Friendly Street continues to grow stronger.

Early this year, when the Box Factory suddenly closed, it was hard to imagine the group would bounce back so quickly. Many of the members had been going to the Box Factory from the very beginning. There were countless memories tied in the building; in the very way the wooden stairs creaked. The move came as a shock, and the pangs of nostalgia are still present. Months later, Friendly Street is flourishing in its new home, the Writers' Centre. Unlike bricks and cement, the shared passion that holds Friendly Street together can't ever be knocked down. We will always have our words. We will always have our voices. Memories, too, cannot be destroyed. Meanwhile, we are creating new ones. Friendly Street still attracts new members every month; they are always encouraged with a loud and – of course – friendly clap. We were all in that situation once, after all.

The poems of this year's anthology reflect the spirit of Friendly Street's members. There's sorrow there, frustration, hardship, and fear, reflecting the often unstable world we live in. Underlying it all, however, is an undeniable strength: the determination to live and love at all costs; this is why human beings need poetry; this is why Friendly Street thrives.

Enjoy.

Amelia Walker and Shen

Adelaide

In the shopping mall

a businessman
is riding
a fat brass pig.

A pigeon eats steak off the pavement

Everyone has forgotten what to do

A woman in a suit wails to be fed

The mayor skewers
five cent cans into a hessian bag
with the spoke from a bicycle

Anti-peace protestors march to
the steps of parliament house

All white people live in the park

Parking inspectors give themselves tickets
every time they step in a crack

Pensioners are paid to play poker machines

The premier lives in a tree

Michael Kingsbury

Want

I want
   to hang on your lip
      like that cigarette
   you just rolled
and set alight
      *

   the way you drew
            hard
      as if life, or death,
   depended on it
and dragged its smoke
         down into your chest
            then let it escape
               . . . satisfied . . .
      from your throat
      *

   I want
      to be that rich tobacco
         when you can't resist
      its open pouch
must thrust
   your nose in
      for the aroma it exudes.
      *

I want
   to know that artistry
            of thumb and finger
               that passionate restraint
         the long lick
   of preparation.
      *

I want
   to burn
      my insides to ash
         in your embrace.
      *

And when
I have entered your body
                    disguised
                            as your breath
                I want
            to rise again
                    with that next cigarette
                            fire up in your fingers
            the slow burn of addiction
making us want
                and want
                    and want.

Deb Matthews-Zott

Nipples

(for Honey G)

Nipples are not on-off buttons
they are radio dials waiting to be tuned in.
Nipples are not raisins
they are glace cherries on frosted cup cakes.
Nipples are not freckles
they are beauty spots on powdered cheeks.
Nipples are not rivets
they are marshmallows to roll on the tongue.
Nipples are not bulldogs
they are seal-point Siamese, soft and strokeable.
Nipples are not beans
they are chocolate stars, caramel buds, aniseed rings.
Nipples are not pebbles
they are lustrous pearls glistening in the shower.
Nipples are not shy
they are brave Sherpas leading women on journeys.

Jude Aquilina

Tilbury Docks – June 1968

she stood alone in the milling crowd
her pulse a caged bird fluttering
her heart painted battleship grey

the giant white floating castle
cast shadows from empty porthole eyes
the yawn of its decks engulfed those

who sought a better life
in the land of milk and honey
in the lucky country

eager groups of migrant stick figures
swarmed over decks and stairwells
three of the waving arms her closest family

streamers flowed from eager hands
as the ship creaked away from the dockside
severing the tenuous umbilical cord

she stared wordlessly at the watery space
made wider still by her salty tears
and the iron band tightening around her heart.

Jill Gower

To my donor

Your lungs have found a home
Next to my heart.
My heart goes out to your family,
As broken hearts depart, yet
Act strong in the belief that the gift
Of life is your saving grace;
Their precious memories safe,
As life goes on through you,
A sweet breath of fresh freedom
For the precious young woman
As I know you to be, I breathe
Through you, we are intimate
You are close to my heart,
I love you.

Kingsley Whittenbury

Anatomy chart

Are you my mirror, my MRI?
Dissected on the wall, flensed diagram
badged with Latin labels, manikin
flayed for my inspiration and instruction,
your bundled muscles dry as Sunday mutton,
you show me how I work, but never why.

The artist allowed you a fleshed Alice band,
full ears and lips. Your narrow hips
and the hang of your arms
mark you as a male, and your tight-clenched fists.
Spread palms are extras
for this man-map with spare parts,
GM freak, factory-farmed,
packed with choice-cut cameos:
leg, rump, belly, foot and arm.
Bring on the parsley sprigs
for my spare-rib Romeo.

Yet muscle doesn't make the man.
Your pumping city throb –
its freeways, tunnels, arteries – is gone.
Did you ever have a heart? Did you ever read Donne?
And if its true – and he should know –
Love's mysteries in souls do grow
But yet the body is his book
you're a hard read, *Homo liber*,
and I'm stuck.

You're a mystery thriller with the last page gone.
You're a censored letter from the front.
You're an empty wetsuit surfing
when the owner's out for the count.
You're the Aral without the sea,
and a map of *some* of me.
but you won't be the whole me, ever.
And though metaphor wears thin
and cliché runs like a river
I've got you under my skin.

Patricia Irvine

7

My mother's Head

My mother's head is made from stone

My siblings grow themselves
With vulgar intention, upwards
Saplings: brothers, sisters all
They stand, indifferent
& push upwards for the sky

My father is headless
Walks his body through the house
Quietly from room to room
Purpose has fallen down into his legs
Marked daily with little sounds: slippers on carpet

I do not know how to speak
My tongue belongs to my grandfather

We have been cut out of the living will
Of my mother

In this house
There is way too much tea being made
Far too many times a day
The doors are opened and shut
And words do not survive long
In this atmosphere

My mother's head is made of stone
My father is headless

My sister sighs, asks things, quietly, only of herself
In her little closed-door square
She is planning her escape

The dog is a tree now too

Even its intention
Is a straight line from here.

Kim Mann

Suburbia rules

1.
If your children aren't hearing you
its because you are not yelling loud enough.

2.
The best things in life are quite expensive.

3.
When choosing a vehicle, think accident, think children
4WDs are by far the safest:
children will bounce off them with hardly a smudge.

4.
The homeless. They want to harm you.
They want your stuff.
And think about it. There are more of them every day.
They are your enemy. Destroy their nests.

5.
If your life is to be rich and filled with parties and friends
you will need a very big house with en suites and a spa.
Build it and they will come.

6.
For max. classiness
try planting iceberg roses
in perfect straight lines.

7.
It is your duty to perform random acts of senseless shopping.
This is why you have been working for all these years.

8.
Cyclist are losers. Pedestrians are the lowest of the low.
They have chosen life in the slow lane. How can they
expect to get ahead with such a negative attitude?
Do not be hard on them; they deserve your pity.
Demonstrate your generosity and patience by giving way to them
but only if they smile.

9.
A large assembly of youths will invariably orchestrate
the overthrow of liberal democracy
and the destruction of our hard-won rights and freedoms.
Call the police without delay.

10.
Native gardens lead to
- unsightly loss of streetscape symmetry
- drain-blockage caused by leaf-droppage
- automatic contamination by avian manure
- highly venomous snake infestation
- possible death through falling limbs
If you detect native gardens in your area,
report them to your council. They are un-Australian.

11.
Alarm your house, alarm your car,
alarm your boat, alarm your dog.
But do not alarm yourself.

12.
Water is a valuable resource and belongs to us all.
Be considerate. Hose your driveway down at night
when water restrictions do not apply.

13.
Palm trees are the go.

14.
Avoid eye contact with your neighbours.
You never know when they may become homeless.

15.
These suburbs are under continual surveillance.
Have a nice day.

Peter Manthorpe

At the centre

At the centre there is a still core
We will always be kids sitting in the hayfield
in a private world, the tall

grasses feathery with flower, bending
over us, through which we glimpsed
a blue sky unending

where the hovering larks would soar
until they were almost as small
as sandflies and would pour

out their high notes almost beyond reach
of even young ears. The warm straw
and soil lulled us, until we each

found we had nothing more to say
complete in our friendship
feeling this was eternal, this day.

Rae Sexton

Parting with a friend

(for Graziella)

Who would have thought the border
between two countries would lie in
a suburban fence on common ground
where we would meet; that you

would take my Celtic cloak, paint it
with colours from the Adriatic Sea
and partner me with music
when I dance on Cornish moors.

Day by day we weave
enduring patterns with our threads,
you weft my warp together,
made firmer by the shuttle

of our passage back and forth
through friendship's gateway,
whose hinge, like a horizon,
holds us fast.

But now it's time to say goodbye,
so you take the earth and I'll take the sky.

Jill Gloyne

Coffee

We had a trial separation,
coffee and I.
We just weren't working out.
We were relying on each other
and I'd forgotten who I was.

I'd had enough of the demands,
the persistent needs.
It needed me
to justify its existence.
I needed it to feel alive.

The anger came
late one night.
I was desperately grid-locked at every angle
by countless pressures and deadlines.
I embraced the warm flow of coffee.

The heat in my hands,
the steam caressing moisture on my nose,
I gave in to my life-giving comforter.
And I became horribly awake,
totally aware of my disintegrating situation.

I couldn't think.
I couldn't concentrate.
Unwelcome thoughts mushroomed
into pressing concerns. Until:
the defiant anger of the resurfacing soul.

So we broke up for a while.
It was better that way.
Until one morning.
I had been staring at the TV for hours,
and a new realization emerged.

We were living a lie.
I was not really living.
Just lazily floating in my body
waiting for a thought to arrive.
Wasting every beautiful, fresh morning.

Breathlessly I made a cup,
I hadn't realized until that moment
just how much we missed each other.
A jar labeled *Coffee* now has been placed by the kettle,
and we now get up early to watch every sunrise.

Andre Starr

Speaking in tongues

When we speak in tongues
Your words slide
Wet and wild
Down my throat

When we speak in tongues
My words pour out
And fill you up
Like water

When we speak in tongues
Your words ride
My saliva
To wider rivers

When we speak in tongues
My words melt
Like chocolate
And dissolve like sugar

When we speak in tongues
We speak with eloquence
And muscle
And silent insistence

When you speak to me with your tongue
You fill my mouth
With sense
And I can't answer back

When I talk to you
With my tongue
I say
I love you.

Judy Dally

Olives

Wet loam, bare vines, grey olive trees,
the sky blue-cold. Its cloudy fretwork
shadows Lyndoch ridge.
Kestrel and wedgetail winch in wind,
alert to cryptic prey.
Laurasia's rabbit and Gondwana's skink
alike are food to them,
spread on the valley's chequered tablecloth
where earth is never border, only edge.

We lay our nets beneath the olive trees,
dislodge green galaxies, black planets,
the seasonal, returning gifts
of aliens now rooted deep and strong
as red gums by the creek.

They're all alike. Pick any one.
Now bite. Black bile, tongue-bane!
You gag on bitter alien skin.
Yet in their press of thousands
they yield what loneliness withholds, locks in.
Their chrism makes our table rich,
our bread, our lives green-gold.

Patricia Irvine

pixel nervosa

your digital camera
allows your eating disorder
to soar to new heights

you capture food in pixels
create jpegs of your breakfast
      bitmaps of lunch
      gifs of dinner

your pc's menu
takes on
an entirely new meaning

later
you binge
in a slideshow of courses
meals flash across your screen
in
calorific technicolour

you savour each morsel
as it slips
      past
      and down
      and through

you're fit to burst
stretched to server capacity
temporarily sated

until
remorse sets in
and
the download begins

at ten megabytes per minute
it takes seventeen seconds
to move the entire contents
of your stomach
to the recycle bin

Rachel J Manning

electric love

something about turning thirty made men more attractive – and I mean – any man – as long as they were upright and warm – I wanted them – I wanted them all the time – but – with the risk of disease or unwanted pregnancies ever present I decided to go electric. I bought a vibrator – it would double as a massage tool – the extremely young sales rep. at the sexy lingerie party told us – we all bought one – to massage our shoulder – we said. I tried it as soon as I got home – but it got hotter as I got colder – I tried it in all sorts of positions – it began to smoke – sparks flew – then it exploded – giving me a frightening jolt – but no release. I gave up electric love.

G M Walker

Versatility

My genitalia are unique.

I have three detachable penises
which screw into a brass socket
three centimeters above my scrotum:
lubricated, fully articulated, irrigated,
with all necessary sensory connections.

The first a veritable maypole
painted in a spiral pattern
of green, blue and silver
with a helmut in fire engine red:
displayed on request at festivals,
pageants, writers weeks
and similar events.

The second a camouflaged modesty
with my regimental badge affixed:
always concealed but comforting
on Anzac Day and army reunions.

The third an impressive erection
bronzed, with pronounced veins,
stabilized by four silken guyropes
attached to my trouser belt:
and which
I trot out
whenever
I need
to make
an utter
prick
of
my
self.

Ray Stuart

and after

The melting breathing night
started by hands and continued by tongues
you were so pale
me HAH I was a hero

but the melting weeping night
sorted by strands and contended by stars
your hair a medusa
me BAH I was a god

but the meeting leaping night
clung and flung so close
walking home in the rain
sheltering in each other

it was not the moon who asked
or even the raggedy clouds
you just glowed
me AH I was like the drowned

and after, well it was the touch
of your hand that was the warmest
of all.

Avalanche

There is more ...

Of course there is more
Beyond the mountains that encircle the village
Beyond the capsule of the suburban street

Of course there is more
Outside perception, invention and every dusty paradigm
reflection, projection and every hackneyed measurement
model, make-over and every collected memory

Of course there is more
Behind the cloak of the stellar host
Beneath the earthen belly and watery grave
Between our illusions, mimicry and misadventures

Of course
there is more . . .

Geoff Johnston

the architecture of birds

exposed by a broken branch
the nest sails to earth
as though on a parachute

it was not designed for flight
but such is its strength
that it lands unbroken

I lift it gently, a cup of twigs
examine the way beak has bent
each thread of grass
      each twig, thin as a hair
woven expertly around the other

the way the nest is layered
each intricate piece knitted into place

even the smallest human hands
could not manage such delicate work

and at its centre, a cotton softness
wisps of lint, fragments of fabric
stolen from washing lines, rubbish bins

pinned to the wall's curve is a single leaf
like an antique on the mantelpiece
an emblem of bird domesticity

I find a new home for this home
imagine two eggs of sky
      cradled in its hollow

two tiny children held safe
in the palm of a mother's hand

Graham Catt

Jordy's balloons

after the funeral
outside to inevitable
sun

            watching his eight year old mates release purple/
              white balloons shrinking into a perfect blue sky

a week's
grieving
spent

 relieved children smiling laughing faces upturned sunflowers seeking
   light   warmth   celebrating his life   intent eyes on diminishing orbs

but on
fear-engraved
faces

            the aching eyes of every parent on their own
          child   seeing them disappear in an instant

like balloons.

Rob Walker

grief

first my face started to harden
crack – crumble
I watched as my nose fell
shattered into dust
no blood
the wind swirled the dust
of myself around me
until I was just two eyes
a few bits of teeth
in a maelstrom of dust

G M Walker

nickie

she slips through the cracks, unnoticed,
its not called the road less travelled for no reason.
trying to be cool like a new york model
but ending up a splat avocado
linking road kill and destiny
punch drunk and without bail
vomit as words spewing from her lips
knowing there'll be consequences
wishing there'd be silence
hoping there's more strength
feeling the strange inside, but not knowing
where all this hurt is coming from.
all she has is red edged eyes and deaf angel.
does death smell like vinegar?
Is this why doves cry?

Kerryn Tredrea

The ache within the light

At first the pain in her head
is sly and approaches from the side,
withdraws if she tries to look.
There are momentary flashes –
like cat's eyes widening
in nocturnal surprise.

Later, a faint sparkle holds
the edge of her vision –
as if a sheer and glittering
curtain is being drawn in
slowly from off-stage. It dots
every movement beyond
with light, haloes them
with an unholy aura.

When she closes her eyes,
she begins to see bright flecks
on black, imprints of stars
on the undersides of her lids.

Later again, though she lies
in her darkened room,
the light is all there is –
a huge mirror in which she sees
only herself, hands cupped around
her now-pounding head,
fingers spread and opened
as if cracks on a delicate vase.

Shen

Autistic child in classroom

Fiercely she rocks back and forth
as if trying to push out a word

Instead managing only
a few murmurs
or the occasional sentence of sounds

Frustrated she bites into her own forearm

Before running with the force
of a meteor falling

Mostly
she speaks in touch with her fingertips
which she is continually redrafting
till

Someone gets the message

Jules Leigh Koch

For Melanie she has her cell

How cleverly she builds her cell
And lays upon its floor a mat
Of fragrant rush, how very well
She's spelled her cot; there's too a cat
That keeps her company. She's lots
Of cider, stored in seven crocks,
Tart apples, nuts, sweet honey pots,
White tallow lamps and candle clocks;
Against the dark she does her work,
For though the days are sunny bright
There's Older Powers, and Things Which Lurk;
And soon will prowl the Secret Night:

But she'll be snug, as we can tell,
For Melanie she has her cell.

George Woolmer

Bury me in my bathing suit

When I die don't cast me into another plot
confine me to another box.
All my life
I have been boxed in spaces,
certain places for certain occupations.

For once let me be free to fly without restriction.
Cast me out into the
so-black slow black, blue black,
iridescent night,
to cavort with stars and angels.

When I die don't set me to lie in an appropriately
dignified garden,
amongst old biddies
who think they own the place because they died last century.
Don't leave me amongst an artificial garden,
amongst those still crying for their own deaths.
Forever a place of mourning,
lost memories, lost possibilities.

For once I would like to be infinitely inappropriate.
Bury me in my bathing suit with bright red lipstick
and sparking red high heels
that are amazingly uncomfortable
for I won't have to walk anywhere in them.

Let my breath escape me, no longer confined to this body
let it dance a jig
like dust mites in a stream of sunshine,
no longer a prisoner to my lungs
being pulled in and out and in again.

When I die cut out my heart
and give it to someone else for a while
let it boom boom boom
out another life.
There's love in the old ticker yet.

When I die don't mark the spot with a heavy
lump of polished granite.
Don't hold my head down with the weight of my life
rather, let X mark the spot
an indicator of a buried treasure,
a steamy lot of seedy stories,
a cheeky grin and a glint in the eyes.

When I die let me burn and flicker amongst flames.
Let me evaporate and disappear into the air,
a crafty magician.

Let me float to the very edge, the point between earth and sky,
    sky and space,
to the honky tonk of a jazz band and a raucous party,
so all my friends
all my family
drunk as skunks
will remember my death in the foggy glow of the morning after
and no tears will dampen my exit.

Alyssa Sawyer

Sabi*

It was her dress I remember –
the flowers, the faded charm.
Imagine a cottage garden
shadowy with wisteria,
the mauve spilling, the green.

Surrounded with patterns –
pinstripe, check, plaid –
that dress stepped out quietly.
It had a calm of its own.
As the old lady passed me
with a slight nod of her head,
purple blossom scattered.
There was perfume in the air.
I sense leaves unraveling,
petals adrift at her hem.

Elaine Barker

*in Zen philosophy, the love of old and faded things

Night of the broken glass fingers
for Celina

'twas a night of broken glass fingers
splinters stuck up veins   &   a maelstrom for a room –
burning your baby body with melting linoleum
& charring your face with the ashes
another night of head smashing tongue lashing gashed love
another night of fate worn cries of helpful hopelessness
in this   pooling   down
another night reaching for God in the Sistene Chapel
standing the breath between the fingers
on the fresco of The Creation
& receiving a copy of *The Power of Positive Thinking*
revised edition   by   Samuel Beckett
another night tying nooses on escape routes
in a sweet attempt to aid the other in flight-fright
standing atop the cliff   jumping   shouting
I'm free   *I'm free!*
another night reaching for Love   &   finding it
in the blender
weeping caustic soda
saying   *this glass is empty*   *CRUSH IT!*
but   you   know   you'd   only   have   to   sweep   it   up
& bandage
your   hand
the sun is coming   what   do   they   say?
today
is   the
first   day
of the   rest
of your   life.

Glen Murdoch

the other woman

i grasp the life jackets you offer
  calls that ring in my hallway
  flowers that fill my lounge

i cling to them in frenzy
and confront myself with options
  hold on
  hoping your ship will collect me
  let go
  peacefully and silently slip under

i thrash about
panic when i loosen my grip
afraid of the cold darkness
my only achievement to date
has been the attraction of sharks

  i wish i were a stronger swimmer
  i wish you were a better navigator

perversely i'm glad we're not
in this current
i don't have to make a choice

i can reserve my flares
for another wreck

Rachel Manning

smile don't frown
woman trouble
is simply the best kind

what writing career is this
sending away for rejections?

Kon Kalembakis

Beach haiku

Summer afternoon
the sea hushing and shushing
dreams into evening

A small white feather
fragile as any human
stranded on the shore

Maeve Archibald

Symmetry

With tears in his eyes
she waves him from her life
she has gone – moved on

He is cut down the middle
the only perfect thing left
is the symmetry in which
he has been sliced
two perfect halves – the same
each now reflecting the other
where before he reflected her
and she reflected him

He is left squatting on memories
looking left and right
trying to see his conciousness
from a different angle
everywhere he looks – he sees
himself in mirror image

For three long years
he only sees himself
reflected in the mirror

that is his separation from self
then she calls him and
tells him that she wants him back
and gives him the very key
that unlocks the door
that sets him free
and makes him whole again

With tears in his eyes
he waves her from his life
he has gone – moved on.

Iain Spalding

Poem for the woman in the mangroves

1.
The loom of day wraps itself around you,
unfurls to an hour where the sun stands still,

high above your nakedness.

In my ears, a rousing call
and the sound of walls falling.

2.
Tiny crabs scuttle away before our feet.
Bubbles of air pock the water's surface.

The mangroves lie low, huddling to their shadows,
keeping to themselves.

Your head, your uplifted arms, break the horizon.

3.
The clay is soft and cool beneath our toes,
between our fingers.

We spread streaks aross our skin,
rivers running aground, drying in the sun.

Unnoticed, the tide goes out.

4.
We stand apart, leaning toward each other,
arms raised high. Our hands touch

forming a doorway into the sky.

5.
We stand together, back to back,
palms facing each other behind our necks.

I cannot see you, yet I see you.
You do not speak to me, yet you speak to me.

Language floats in the space around us,
in the spaces between us.

6.
Adrift in the shallows, your pale body,
a white island in a green mangrove sea,

mooring place for my eyes.

7.
You have closed your eyes
and lie back in the water with arms outstretched.

The sun shines upon you.
The wind sends ripples of water against you.

Quietly, so as not to disturb, my heart sings.

8.
You wash the clay from my back.
I turn, scoop water over your neck

and shoulders, your ridged spine.
Beneath my hands your back glistens.

Above and around, the air shimmers.

David Ades

Speech of parts

I don't know what I metaphor.
I tried ten puns to make her laugh.
             No pun intended.

I'm a poet   I ejaculated   prematurely –
She just left me   dangling

a participle, part-disciple, part-adieu, pas de deux
cut me to the Quink with her secateurs
             (non-sequitur)

my heart cut up as a found poem
split   as an infinitive

I am in the present   tense
she,   the past,   perfect

Rob Walker

The light of reality

Trips to the circus are no longer fun
in adulthood. I see beyond the show
to peeling paint, costumes worn and yellow
with age. Faces below the greasepaint
are tired from bills and faking cheer.
My pulse shudders
as the juggler adds another plate. He metamorphs
and then it's me beneath the glare.
An audience of friends and strangers waits;
wants and needs one plate of mine to drop
work, food, money, kids, relationship.
One aspect of my life to smash
out of control will deflect the other's eyes
from their miseries and spills.
Another youthful favourite
holds no more delight. The gypsy lady
hunched over her divining ball. She promises
no future with a hero and a lottery prize.
Even if her crystal were genuine not fake,
only the last can have that rosy coloured glow.
Tomorrow reflect her face, wrinkles the horizon,
greys the day as reality blooms and dreams fade.
My life will be reduced to a hole
in muddy ground . . .
There's no running away to join the circus now
and no more belief in clowns.

Martina Taeker

My first bath with a girl

I remember my first bath with a girl.

Blue walls, white tiles
with seaweed, a deep
green, soapy tub.

Was I four?
She was, too.

When I asked
where her thing like mine was
she knelt and turned
her shiny
wet bottom round

I remember thinking it was all
very beautiful.

She farted in my face and dived.

Richard Tipping

Queen Victoria's diary

In her diary
the young wife
Queen Victoria
liked to watch
every stroke of
Albert's shaving.
As far as it's
possible to know
it's not known
whether or not
the young husband
Prince Albert
liked to watch
every stroke of
Queen Victoria's
shaving or
whether she shaved
at all. It's
equally uncertain
whether the shaving
or not shaving
the watching or
not watching
the recording or
not recording
had more impact
on the rise or
on the fall of
the British Empire.

Graham Rowlands

At Warriparinga

Gateway to the Tjilbruke Dreaming

Great tree trunks
mark the site – aged,
gashed, scarred, grey, worn.

Rusting clasps and chains
bring our past into this present
but the Kaurna shield is here.

A spear high
above the tallest tree
points toward dawn.

A sacred ibis
wing-tips spread
turns south.

Wood smoke rises
from this winter fire
fed by old roots.

Boys play around
the ritual flames
flickering in wind.

A seven-year old
nephew / son stands
at his uncle's knee.

His young breath
powers a didgeridoo
waking his land and us.

Erica Jolly

I was Clifford Possum Tjapaltjarri's Auntie

for a short sixty minutes,
within the magic of your exhibition,
my 'nephew',
where your multitudinous dots
danced and sang in rhythmic call.
Your spirit whisked mine away.

You smiled,
proud,
from your photo,
my 'nephew',
your black face a grin.
Were you astonished at your 'auntie's' skin colour – Celtic white –
and pleased with the conspiracy?
(The white lady attendant, when told,
'This is Clifford's auntie',
widened her eyes at me, handed me an entry token,
dumb.)

I slipped free
into the worlds of your dots, colours and energy,
my 'nephew',
honoured to be of your clan,
wishing it could last forever;
our Dreaming.
Reconciliation.

Alice Shore

Seeing in the New Year

(for Mary Falkland 1940–2004)

The fireworks from the party still
smoking in the city distance
the slowest New Year's Eve ever.

You die on New Year's Day at 1.40 am.
How did you arrange this Mum?
an optimist's death . . .
breathing on into a new year

. . . clouds,
as slow as your death,
obscure the moon.
A possum hurtles itself
into the pittosporum tree
Outside the house is illuminated
with your shimmering spirit.

I sit and listen
for signs of you
freeing yourself from this world.
The house breathes, creaks, sways, groans,
like the death within it . . .

Your skin becomes gossamer tissue
holding you ever more slightly in this body.
Touching my hand, your fingernail
scratches me by accident

I'm sorry I hurt you Jo
you say

and the spaces inside my heart,
all darkness and fragments of light
open out into a universe of forgiving.

Joanna Falkland

Star webs

Withered red skirts
of bottlebrush
tangle in yesterday's
spider web
woven in front of
the side mirror

that reflects
urban landscape
shop verandahs
stone villas and roses.

Webs enmesh beauty
tangle birth
catch stars that dazzle sunrise.

Margaret Fensom

Skin flowers red

beyond the cactus bloom
beneath the pyramid bed
of the shrouded citadel
where angels walked
                    the zocalo

my eyes scale the plaza
in the abandoned axis
of the final sleep

Lidija Simkute

In darkness and silence

below houses of ochre
and apricot
stirs the underworld

Mayan signs
of ritual shadows
in sacrificial ruins

connects us to the gods

their intricate dance
the roots of life and death

Lidija Simkute

Lone Pine Legacy

(It is believed that Anzac troops at the Battle of Lone Pine brought back
seeds from that particular tree to plant in Australia)

Those seeds from the first Lone Pine
that the Anzacs wanted to plant in us
have changed . . .

They were chopped up by Maxim fire
somewhere in the Somme;
smothered in phosgene clouds, broiled by mustard gas
in the fetid muck of Passchendaele;
shredded to shards by high explosives on Vimy Ridge;
eviscerated on the wire at Ypres Salient.

Those seeds changed all right – they had to.
But the men who'd harvested them
in the Dardanelles and brought them safe
through France and Palestine
intended a new planting,
a different destination, in unsullied
fresh soil.
These soldiers simply wanted peace.
No more Lone Pines,
        Sari Bairs
        Shrapnel Gullies
        or any more
of the lunatic tragedy of the Western Front
ever ever ever
again.

It didn't happen quite
as they'd hoped.
The seeds were planted though –
planted and tended by people who hadn't been
to Lone Pine
or any of the other places.

These men and women – in political office,
in always spotless military uniform,
in a thousand flag-saluting, anthem-braying, drum-thumping
ceremonies said:
    'War's OK. After all, it's about
preserving freedom,
saving democracy,
the Australian way of life,
decency,
Christian values,
the Empire,
and – of course –
ensuring eternal PEACE . . .
So let's keep at it,
and make sure the appropriate soil
is ever-prepared . . .'

Thus the seeds survived and grew
in generations coming after Anzac.
they germinated – in heads and hearts and souls,
put down roots –
gnarled, twisted, blackened roots
which turned their bearers twisted too.

The pine trees grow, for good or ill,
they've grown tall, are growing still.
And the generations coming, friend –
what seedlings will they plant and tend?

Geoff Hastwell

the wounded city

the moon is broken, the clouds are bleeding

the city skyline is missing some teeth

the sidewalks are stained with neon and shadow

I tread carefully
     stepping between puddles of light

I avoid smouldering cars, a shop grafittied with blood, a row of tanks

I pass the ruins of a supermarket
     its bones licked clean by tongues of fire

I pass a derelict hospital, a boarded-up cinema

I see a crowd gathered in the ribs of a cathedral
     the sound of the choir is an anaesthetic

I hear the rattle of gunfire, a jet fighter puncturing the sky

I see soldiers on street corners
      a dead dog hanging from a lamppost

I see shoppers and office workers rushing home in the dark

the moon is fractured, the moon is made of glass

pale lights drip from the eye-sockets of skyscrapers

there is a man-shaped hole in the night

  I am walking through it

Graham Catt

Fat Boy Blues

This moon's no fingernail
but a plate
I'd like to eat off
This Greek china's overwhelming

But I always manage
with ease and relish
and anger welling
repetition is the mainstay

Apathy's mine
– the how big can I get then?
Syndrome.
This big and then some.

Always room for more
and I love her
squeeze it in for your sake
but there's always tomorrow

Yes there's always tomorrow

Peter Tsatsoulis

Lady Macbeth

She was never very good
at knitting without a pattern –
and now she's lost it.

Her problem lies between
the stitch she dropped and guilt
at having to unravel a sleeve
that will not be cast off.

Her grand design has tied her
into knots she can't undo
to wash away the stain
of blood-red needles.

Sweet sleep, for her, will never
die a natural death again.

Jill Gloyne

Line

moist
fever
subsiding
spasms
around
midnight
on
the brink
of sleeping

Dhora Moustrides

Newborn

Hurt by the harsh glare
of electric lights, the eyes
flinch, are drawn back
to the dazzle of a new sensation
where knowledge is pain
then involuntarily retreat

to peep out like a primeval
stirring of life in watery sand
or to sleep on in a dark world
of soothing ignorance

I see in your slitted eyes
something of our origin
long since erased
from our memory
lodged at the darkest end
of sight.

Ros Schultz

Up

Once the sun shuts up
It gives the other stars a chance
In deepening sky
I lie on a backyard trampoline and watch

Pin-pricks through rubber/ A bicycle tube stretched
The camera obscura sustained flesh/ On timeless delay
Curtains and boxes
Or someone shifting a torch behind
A perhaps hand perhaps eye looking through

David Mortimer

The reluctant bride

I was promised, they said
but when they came
I found an attic box
just big enough to hide me
until all had left
then I fled over rooftops
clambered down a walnut tree –
the back fences, roads, fields,
the next town, a train, a ship
days and breathless days
I ran and ran

I slept in cellars and under stars
I slept in frosted orchards
by the glow of smudge-pots
I changed my name and dyed my hair
I learnt a new language
I dressed as a boy
I wore a tattoo
I worked on road-gangs
I traded skins
that made me three fortunes I lost
then I set out beyond the camps and houses
beyond the world of man

there I ate wild fruit and small lizards
I fought with lions and a red moon
then where skies turn a roiling mass of blue
where birds live underground and fish in air
I stopped running –
I built a house from mud and sticks
bred honey bees
grew pears
and stayed

six years safe
and here he comes again
his steps are less sure
and without his clamouring entourage
but I know that grin –
I'll stand at the doorway
in my own rough finery to greet him
and this time
maybe
I'll just say No.

Steve Evans

Ineligible

Once again the vernal bachelors have passed.
I am not so denim as the chosen ones who dip
their lovely fingers in, nor do I know
how to command a man and his socks. Furthermore,
my father has left me a dowry of unpleasant things.
Once I tried to walk where twelve roses would snare my hem.
I met odd shapes and other sunkenfolk.
A blank man stole my cherries. Then one spring day
I met myself and disappeared in dust from my shelf.

Libby Angel

Remember me

Let the impression that I leave behind,
linger
playful and compelling.
Let thoughts of me flash through her mind,
splash light upon concealed regret.
She held me in hands cupped tight
let me slide between her fingers
with exquisite care,
as some iridescent beetle,
shiny and sleek,
too precious to hold
she had no heart to keep me there.
I had to go
although I knew
and still know
I was never safer than in her hands.
This I also know
this unraveling,
this letting go
as hard for her as it was for me.
We are all insects
scurrying in search of safe haven,
we might have found it in each other's arms,
but if our clinging together could not be
all I ask
is she remember me.

Kate Alder

Careless joy

You walked in that morning, casual and buoyed,
'She's going up' – you meant the mountain and you
Meant the truck cum caravan, home-made
House-high and heavy – we drinking tea,
Wintering in sun, next thing caroling
Up the track, you with a grin like ignition,
Wallowing in momentum, Sarah calling
'O my life', going for the door – the hairpin
Would have us over with the weight, the blood
Was in our heads – cranked-up and on a spree,
You swung us up to the top: it was careless joy
And single-mindedness, carried us that day.

Karen Blaylock

Camping Ground Desiderata

Watch sorties of ravens and magpies
as you sip your beer, cooled on ice.
It was a long drive here,
looking for silence and birdsong.

Note how the stony path
holds the range in miniature,
and come to savvy
the strata of things.

See beyond the workday pixels
glows a hill of Spinifex
and another and another.

Hurry with the going of the light
and rise with the rising of it,
feeling patterns of convection,
gully winds at dawn and dusk.

Care about the stars even though
you know they don't care about us.
Name them with a platonic love,
point out shapes to your children.

Observe even the smallest wren
pegs out its territory.
Feel again a tangible economy
of shelter, fire and food.

Be intimate once more with the dirt:
in your plate, in your hair,
in the loop roads of your guts.
The grime under your nails telling
where we came from and where we go.

Mike Ladd

Camping

'Each year we go camping
in the Flinders Ranges,' says my friend,
'no water, no toilets, canned food –
the dirt, the joy of it.'

> *I wake up in the cold – electricity*
> *needs to be rationed.*
> *Water needs to be rationed –*
> *It comes through pipes*
> *twice a day for two hours.*
> *I save up drinking water,*
> *water to wash my face,*
> *and in the bathroom, in the tub,*
> *I have what I call 'my indoor pool'.*
> *The bathroom is cold.*
> *I freeze when I got to the toilet.*

'Our kids had a shock,' says my friend,
'when they had to go to the toilet
in the bushes, in the cold –
does them good, roughing it, city kids.'

'Just imagine – no shower for nearly a week,' he laughs
> *Just imagine – warm showers*
> *if you're lucky. Finish quickly*
> *so you have time to go to the kitchen*
> *and save drinking water.*

'Just imagine – canned food from the car boot', he says.
> *I boil an egg on the pale flame –*
> *gas is supplied at dawn for an hour.*
> *Seven eggs per month is the ratio.*
> *When I finish them*
> *I eat canned food.*

'Do you enjoy camping?' he asks,
and suddenly I realize that's what it was
back home before the '89 Revolution –
forever camping.

Ioana Petrescu

The Salt-pan

In my heart I belong,
but in my mind
I see
that I am
one of the different ones.

I am an exception.
Special allowances are made for me
so that I can remain
in my own country.

Everything is a battle,
the land
a meal of left overs –
doled out
in cold charity.

'Sorry' comes late –
too much lost,
unclaimable.

The past
is not reconciled with the now . . .
The future is barren
cracked –
a salt-pan
after years of drought.

Anna Stirling Pope

Shades of Green

'My garden must have
colour at all times,
it must be designed
by a professional,' she said
'with flowers in bloom
each month of the year'.

I reply that green
is also a colour
and that from my window
I can see the sombre green
of a lemon-scented gum
the darker hue of the she-oak
tormented by the June wind
the emerald of pasture
after the opening rains
the lime of an elm
with the lighter touch
of bottlebrush leaves
beneath and against
a vivid green horse rug.
I also add that from the window
I can sometimes detect envy.

Ray Stuart

Maths

The numbers blur before my eyes
Like some bizarre pattern
Forming into one
I gaze at them
Trying to figure them out
The numbers begin to dance
Before my tired eyes
Not making any sense
Faster and faster they swirl
Til they are a kaleidoscope
Of numbers and symbols
My brain is dizzy
Racing round and round
Hurting my head
A voice breaks the spell
Pulls me out of my world
'Sinead, Pay Attention'

Sinead O'Shaughnessy

Carmela

As Carmela thumped
the table with both hands
the dust of silence rose
like a cloud of fine flour
until pressed down again
by soft palms which slid
across a bare table cloth
then scrolled from left
to right pinching silence
between fingers and thumbs
incessantly rolling the past
into potato dumplings.

Gaetano Aiello

A Butterfly

red outlined in blue,
wings outspread
tattooed on her ankle –
a scrap of leadlight
glowing between sensible shoes
and floral print.

Cramped in the café,
barricaded by shopping,
the woman sips tea,
has grown past the years
when rebellion was a heady wine,
and yet their ghost still flutters
with such insouciance
that should she glimpse it one evening
in a certain light, could well believe
she had wings again.

David Cookson

Housework

Fold the plates away
Iron the benchtops
Measure the clothes on the line

Shave the carpets
Exercise the rubbish
Escort the dog off the premises

Drown the dishes
Spreadeagle the quilt
Re-introduce old vegies into the wild

Rinse the garden
Fence with cobwebs
Discipline clothes with the machine

Peel the bathroom
Steal from the hens
Paint images of self on all shiny surfaces

Repeat
Repeat
Repeat

Rachael Mead

Happiness

There's a mortgage on happiness –
you try to rent for a while
but he says those are emotions down the drain.
A mortgage is more solid, you have the illusion of arriving

in thirty years. And you choose between Simpson
and Fisher and Paykel to launder your impatience,
and you carpet the road to your feelings
with rugs advertised on Channel 10.

In the first five years you pay for the carport, the front lawn,
and the rose buds your romantic heart gnaws at
like a possum. You invent a pouch to keep your thoughts safe inside
just like this marsupial who shits all over the front lawn.

And, of course, the bank owns it all.

Ioana Petrescu

Bread and Cigarettes

The Man
His skin is pale.
He opens the curtains
sometimes.
Inside his house
he eats toast
and smokes cigarettes.
He goes out
sometimes
to buy bread
cigarettes
and cat food.
He wishes he could
get them
from a vending machine.

The House
Kitchen
Bedroom
Toilet
Shower
Curtains

The Cat
Siamese sleek
she makes little
flicks of her tail
catches rats
rejects his offerings.
She sometimes sleeps
curled up, almost
making him believe
she is not cruel.
She sometimes demands
to sleep in his bed
(a futon)
when she wants to
on his pillow.

After such nights
he wakes unable
to turn his neck. However
after such nights
he wakes having slept.

Letters
Electricity Bill
Water Bill
Bank Statement
Look 10 Years Younger Overnight!
(conditions apply)
Library Notice:
'I'm Okay, You're Okay'
two years overdue.

Thoughts Running Through His Head On A Sunday Afternoon
I should get out of bed . . .
shouldn't I?
I should.
Why?
Because . . .
I'll only have to
get back in later. If
I get out of bed
I can eat toast.
But I'm sick
of toast. I do
need a cigarette
and a piss.
I wonder where
the cat went last night.
Hope she's okay.
I really should
get out of bed . . .

Items On His Table

Coffee Cup
Ash Tray (overflowing)
Copy of 'I'm Okay,
You're Okay'
(book mark in page nine)
Porno Mag (edges tatty)
Photograph of a woman
with brown hair
green eyes and a gap
between her teeth.

Amelia Walker

Shawl

For Kitty Carlisle

somewhere in Belfast
the young wee girl
under the apron
of her grandmother
soda bread & travel
brochure of grammar
i have never been there
but you were born
in a village the size
of a handkerchief
married to a Royal Welch Fusilier
who returned hairless
from the War
three children later
& the great trip
across the water
ten quid each
& a dinner dance
most nights
all those years
a collection of linen
tea towels rattling
your loneliness
in a flat one street
back from the Gulf
you steamed into
one forty degree day
in February
& have never quite
forgiven yourself
for leaving
except at night
to howl & to cry
for Northern Ireland
a young wee girl
a grandmother
a shawl thrown over
your thin white shoulders.

Rory Harris

Wakening

About an hour I listened to the sea
until the sea was all I heard.
And I watched it climbing
and retreating from the land
as though to carry us away.

But the sea itself was folding
wave on wave, each movement
disappearing like a dream into itself,
upon the wakening of the shore.

And among the crusty scatterings of sea-debris
the wind was laying out the sand
in momentary patterns
of white on ivory.

While all of this dissolved
into the hush of waves, that seemed
the whisperings of static
from a forgotten universe.

Jo Dey

Seascape Memorium

On the dusty track,
Shaded by peeling paperbarks,
I find you waiting
For this, our annual pilgrimage.
All the long, long day,
The wind has torn the clouds into
Swooping kestrel wings.
They race inland over dunes scoured
By southerly squalls.
Perhaps it's only sand grit that
Draws tears from your eyes
And for you his face has faded
From the swirling surf.
Once, we would have braved these waves,
Now, more circumspect,
We watch and wonder why the sea
Chose him and tossed us back.

Annie Ashwell

On the beach

Today
water is wavy
and beach blowy with sand.
Little grains
rushing somewhere

just like us.

Some days
when there is no wind
they just lie there quietly
soaking the sun
taking all the beauty
and peace in

just like me.

The wind.
It blows my hair free.
It whispers and shouts
in my ear.
It rushes somewhere.
Messes up water in the sea.
Seems to have a lot to say.

Be silent for a while.
Stop for a moment
and just be
with me.

Danuta Szot

Rockpool

For Helen D

In the ocean
of your hands
there is a seahorse

Your fingertips are stars
and eyes
are moonstones

Beneath your dress
there is an undertow
and my mouth is the tide

Your words are pebbles
and each promise
is a sunset

Your face has the highs
and lows
of a weather-map

While your body never
gives away
the forecast

When we make love
I close my eyes
to see you

And enter
between dark thighs
your secret rockpool

Jules Leigh Koch

Half Asleep

Even after we've made love
Explicit and explicitly

I notice you hold me

And hope you notice
I hold you

Like we were at a school dance
A quarter century ago

Your arm around my neck
Mine at your waist

Barely a finger
Daring to stray

David Mortimer

My Pirate Daughter

should be crowned captain
of her own ship.
Already she's as fierce,
proud as a prow's carved maiden
talisman for good, or villainy.

No need to raise the jolly roger,
her colours are as clear and
half-mast dangerous
as a broadside ransack.

I wonder at her midnight vigil,
cabin-bound, when all aboard
cradle in their nettled sleep.
What entry will she scrawl
in her logbook journal of the voyage?

Admiral of the besieging fleet
she seeks to elude, I pace
restless through to dawn.
Exclaim, 'Damme, skipped again!'

Somehow, on the lee tide
she's slipped the scudding waves
silent as a dolphin, focused as a shark
beauty, beast, pirate, teen.

Kate Deller-Evans

Shearing

I walk the forty planks
to the end of the shed
rub my pal across
my chin and grab
a bleating skin
and as I lock
the woollen mass
between my knees
I look overhead
to where iron sheets
are pulled back
and blue is framed
by round blackened
oil greased rods
then I trace the cris cross
of beams to the line of
eight green coils
from which spin
electric wheels
driving clipper heads
one of which I grasp
in my own hand
as I spill wool
from sheep
like blankets slipping
from an unkempt bed.

Gaetano Aiello

Pomegranates of Kandahar

Afghan girl
takes her children
takes her few belongings
all that she can carry
always running
to a better place

runs and runs
comes full circle
back to Kandahar
city of pomegranates
shiny blushing skins
encasing countless red cells

she recalls the taste of the
sweet and sour love fruit
each bead unique
each red and succulent
with juices that ooze
between teeth
and run down chins

colouring lips red
like blood running
from the mouth
the blood of Afghans
injured in wars
the blood of Afghans
running over minefields
the blood of Afghan women
stoned to death for
someone else's crimes

love apple
hate apple

nothing has changed

Jill Gower

Lessons From The Rubble

(*Time Magazine*, September 2003. Photograph: The body
of a UN employee in Baghdad is stored in a morgue at a
local hospital.)

Despite the trolley,
the blood-soaked shirt,
the wide channel of blood
that has coursed from forearm to little finger,
this hand is graceful in repose.
The gentle curve of arm and fingers
suggests rest or sleep
speaks, even here, of easy conversation,
music-making, sensuality,
and art.

But the headline has the cold truth.

These fingers, with their silent eloquence,
will never again fasten a button,
brush away a stray crumb,
do any of the other,
thousands of intricate movements,
that make us human,

such as the tender motions of love,
and the assembling of bombs.

Barbara Preston

(Bruce Dawe, in his 1970's poem 'Homecoming',
about Australian soldiers who died in Vietnam, wrote,
'they're bringing them home now, too late, too early'.)

Dear Mr Dawe

I am the boy flown home
from steaming rice fields
cold under the flag

It's been quiet since then
but me and a few good mates
       we battle on
       we do alright

once in a while they dust us off
tart us up for dinner
or a show at the RSL

we look good.
age will not weary us
nor CNN condemn

but Bruce
and here's the thing
old mate
       (I speak for all of us)
       it was always too bloody late.

Nic Rowan

It's Great

SA, South Australia great, Greater Australia great.
Living in Australia is just great, mate, just great.
It's a great place to give football a miss; soccer
rugby union, rugby league & with great determination
I can even give our great Australian Rules a miss
without a sex change operation or being un-Australian.
It might grate but it's great to miss the Grand Final.
Cricket? Australia is a great place to give it a miss
dismissed, missed catches, missed stumps and stumpings
& there's nothing hit & miss about giving it a miss –
no, five days by five times a summer, I go missing in
inaction. Don't even get out of bed. It's great. Great.
I can tell you I've never yet missed missing cricket.
The Sydney to Hobart race is always billed as great.
Maybe. I wouldn't know. When you've seen a rowing boat
you've seen an ocean liner, I always say. Great line, eh?
Of course you & I know it's not always plain sailing.
I can't forget   May Day   May Day   This is May Day &
sailors tossed about like yachts in their great belief
in having a holiday, having a good time. Sad. Tragic.
Almost Rwanda, Kosovo, Chechnya, East Timor, Sierra Leone.
Twice a century the country goes stark staring Olympic
the lead-up all but including & outlasting The Games.
I worked & worked & worked on & out my index finger
in a hard work-out of, well, almost Olympic proportions
& yes, you guessed it – I was turning off my trannie.
When the old Commie weightlifters went for extra lift
they went down a downer. A new test. Hardly uplifting
& not the only ones to go down & stay, I'm sorry to say.
When President Sam's wife went down & stayed (poor old soul)
in the worst possible circumstances (the best Olympics ever)
no one had the heart to repeat the charge of Fascist –
just fireworks here, fireworks there, fireworks everywhere.
No class, no titles – well, fewer and fewer all the time.
Everyone equal to everyone else – well, *someone* else &
the rich serving the poor – occasionally, at Christmas
closely followed down & out by several television crews.
Ah yes! It's a great place, a great country – Australia.

Graham Rowlands

Bee Line

general post office
pie cart on your left
drunk Kaurna your right.

rundle mall
premier shopping district
homeless selling The Big Issue.

parliament house
across King William government house
teens sniffing glue directly ahead.

eds building
office of motor transport
bums picking up cigarette butts.

hindley street west
night clubs and cafes
old men collecting bottles.

welcome to Adelaide
baby sister of Osaka
inequity in progress.

Toby Aikins

Homeless

People who see me
Think I must be cold,
They do not know
The numbness which protects me.

People who see me
Think I must feel shame,
They do not realise
That I am past caring.

People who see me
Look away in guilt,
They think I should not be
What I am.

People who see me
Do not see
That I live in a different world.

Anna Stirling Pope

Neruda, I give you these statues found in the Museum of Port Adelaide …

Each one with its heart still beating
within these walls shaped by time.
In each statue I seek the poem I wrote as a bird took flight.
In the heart of each I read the corn that sailed in boats,
the metal, the flour,
all the dark silk as it made its way across
the destinies of trade.
Each statue bore the sea that stripped it once with its waves,
that washed it free of those dreams sculpted
by hands out of living wood.

Each one has its unmoving heart,
its moon in the night of metals,
its dawn in the ghostly rays
that visit history.
It is you, each surviving statue,
that gives life to these monuments
of city and sea.

The stories of these boats anchored on every wall
are still living in your eyes, sounding out like bells.
They have the passion, the silk, the verses
of the captain who never died,
who was never forgotten.

Figurehead on its bow
piercing through the night of those soldiers
who ravaged your blue kingdom on those shores
where a tyrant was dreaming
of the calm sea of betrayal.

Juan Garrido-Salgado
Translated by Peter Boyle

Neruda te regalo estas estatuas que encontre en el museo de Port Adelaide ...

Cada una tiene su corazón palpitando
Entre los muros del tiempo.
Busco en ella el poema que escribí en el vuelo del ave.
Leo desde su alma el trigo que navegó en los botes;
$\qquad$ Del metal o la harina,
Toda la seda oculta que cruzo los destinos
Del mercado . . .
Cada una tuvo el mar que las desnudo de espuma
Y le lavo todo los sueños que tallaron las manos
De un navegante anclado en la Madera de la vida.

Cada una tiene su corazón inmóvil
Hecho luna entre la noche de los metales
Hecho amanecer entre los rayos de los fantanas
Que visitan la historia.
Son uds, cada estatua que sobrevivio
a la piel y a los monumentos del mar y la cuidad.

La histotria de los barcos anclados en cada muro
Se sostienen en tus ojos de campanas:
Tienen la pasión, la seda y los versos del capitán,
Que no han muerto, ni ha sido olvidado.

Estatua de proa entrando
En aquella noche que los soldados allanaron
Tu reino azul en las costas
De un tirano que soñaba con el mar tranquilo de la traición.

Juan Garrido-Salgado

As One Guise or Another

I was greeted by
An ecstatic, slack jawed
Paper dispenser,
Its sodden torn tongue
lolling into a bashed basin.

The urinal stretched the room,
And despite its stench,
It had a presence,
Like a silent fall,
Or a moat and wall.

The cubicle had no door,
and the pan was seatless,
Stained and encrusted,
But sat unmoved,
Solitary, serene
Like a pagan shrine,
Or a deep still mind.

The concrete floor,
Once dark sea green,
Was stagnant and shallow,
As if evaporation
Had exposed its grey bed.
Around the edges though,
Through floating and congealed
Spittle and phlegm,
Pools of green were still deep
Under a lone electric sun,
Which shone vomit-yellow
Through fly-spots and webs.

But the place
Was strangely comfortable,
In a stoic, even devout way.
There was no shame.
Everything told me,
'We will be transformed,
Already paint has evaporated
And door and seat oxidized.'

And there was a consensus
That until act or accident or entropy
They would wait uncomplaining
In their present state.
For hadn't they been,
And would they be
What are thought, 'Higher' things?
'And aren't we all,'
They called after me,
As I zipped and left,
'Not shat, spat and pissed on,
At one time, or another
In one place, or another,
As one guise, or another?'

Peter Eason

Practical Wisdom

Reality and
subjective reality
are not the same thing.

* * * * *

Exclusionary
over-rationalisation
yields skewed conclusions

* * * * *

Objectivity
is inadequate for our
full understanding.

* * * * *

My beliefs are true
through biological luck
rather than knowledge.

* * * * *

Practical wisdom
lies in decision-making
not talking values.

* * * * *

Not everything is
something from no point of view,
and yet, some things are.

* * * * *

Two alternatives
are incompatible; I
don't exclude either.

This is my claim to knowledge;
this is how I feel the world.

Stephen Lawrence

Standing

standing influences greatly understanding whether
about or still, high or low, within or out, now
or then – particularly if an overview is required
in order that standing, accompanied or not
by understanding, might continue. where
would i have stood when browning was still standing, and
would i have understood? hindsight is a wonderful
thing, but is it possible that standing now i
understand less of what is passing than
that which has passed?
fashion, in or out, is no more or less by force of words
but some are and others aren't fashionable
or so they are made to feel – even by those
without words, a look affirms or destroys
a look, a tune, a book, a meal – a sin
is in or out depending on your standing in the community,
and those who are in or out, of fashion, or sin, or love,
suffer from the same weight of opinion. the
difference is in standing – standing apart
or standing in.

Greg Opie

Ambition

I'd love to write unintelligible poems
Based on the principle of
Obscurity equals depth.
I'd recite them,
And leave everyone wondering
What on earth they were all about . . .
And if I ever became
Well known
Students would have to write essays
On what was really meant
By line one of verse three . . .
Oh well, I try,
But they always come out
In plain simple English.

Garth Dutton

The Head Mistress's Speech

As the school social approaches
it is timely to remind you girls:

No minis, no denim, no platforms.
No gaudy eye make-up nor spidery lashes.
No see-through fabrics. No strapless dresses.
We are not living in Caligula's time.

No G strings. No briefs.
No patent leather shoes
or the boys will see the reflections
from under your dresses.

No liquor. No cigarettes.
And remember
no close dancing – an elbow's
length apart. I will be checking.

And don't let me see you hanging around
giggling all night in the Powder Room.
You must dance. I have taught you all the steps.
You must enjoy the school social.

Jude Aquilina

My First Librarian Was A Greek

And he couldn't speak much English,
but he knew the value of a sixpence.

My first librarian seemed very, very old;
He wore a crumpled dark striped suit,
a heavy silver watch chain looped across his concave middle,
buttoned waistcoat, thin shirt.

He was bent and nervous and twitched a bit
a scraggly iron coloured moustache draped
beneath craggy nose and sucked in cavernous cheeks.

He was my first librarian because he bought books.

Auction lot books: Robinson Crusoe and Marie Corelli
Walter Scott, and The Water Babies;
The Jungle Book, and Peter Pan,
Grubby paperbacks: Raymond Chandler and Peter Cheyney
Dickens and the Brontes; Superman and Batman Comics
Strange books in tiny ancient print, faded covers, and esses for effs:
Books covered in strange waxy brown paper,
Spotted with candle grease; books with loose pages
And split edges:
Some had marbled frontispieces, or were leather bound:
A whole world of riches stacked front edge down in untidy rows
On an old kitchen table on the pavement outside the shop
Half in the sun in a road at the end of which you glimpsed the sea.

The sign above the shop said 'BARBER & WATCHMAKER'

The sign on the table said 'BOOKS 6d'

Sometimes I had sixpence.

I could stand at the table for days
and read every book on it while deciding which one to buy.

Sure, he did chivvy me a little bit.

Then I would buy one
And bring it back the next day,
Saying I didn't like it, and wanted to change it.

Somewhere in that immigrant father in those sad depression years
There surely burned something of the fire of the Greeks of old:

He never chased me away:
And in those days we all knew the value of sixpence.

Betty Collins

Suspendered

In a time of love me do and a hard day's night
I shove my stockings into my school bag
take a short cut home past the Catholic school
envy the nun her habit which
like a Victorian tablecloth
gathering force in the nether regions
and cutting off all comers
between it and the floor
not only protects a well-turned leg
from the lasciviousness of uncouth youth
but also negates the need
to tether stockings to thighs
with a suspender belt which
in the middle of maths
is apt to abandon all sense
of decorum and elasticity
to send a wrinkling
30 denier disaster
scuttling down
said leg
like a rat
down a drainpipe.

Louise Nicholas

SMS

I can make
subtle love to you
with textspeak.

I can
be brave
with abbreviations.

I can
disguise my passion
under acronyms

and only
my lack of dexterity
with the x key

limits
my kisses.

Judy Dally

& into

& into
the heart

of my father
the scratched

out weeds
piled on

dirt paths
where his wife

knelt in
spring time

sowing colour

Rory Harris

Pearls

The heart's ball-bearings
born of an itch –
a stone in the oyster's sole.

Slumped on this page
a trail of moons
cold in the hand
cream of the sea
around a throat that rises throbbing
with life and voice.

Strands handed down from woman
to woman – smooth cheeks of light
a pearl is nothing in the dark.

The moon's nipples
little wheels of love's cart.

Kate Llewellyn

Haiku

Like a red rose you
bloomed from bud to blossom, then
aged to purple tips.

Genevieve Grace Drew

Spring Tide

A full milk-white moon floats in the sky
and I float in your arms
unable to resist the tide.

David Ades

The Gift

That bunch of flowers
took me so by surprise
rekindled the warmth
till the announcement
that we could cut

the bunch in two
and give one half to mother
snap froze my veins
and the chill words
'if you like'
hung in space
like stalactites.

Ros Schultz

Physiology

Chest tightening
releasing
aware of breath
deep breathing
slow heaving
up and down
sound of breath
measure of heart
pounding
rise and fall of breasts
muscle memory
replaying a rhythm
born out of arousal
tactile and thrilling
turned to trembling
to fear this newness
body remembering
the face of a future
devoid of you.

Kate Alder

The Devil

I remember when the devil moved inside me, despite the Jesus at my
breast. The water turned many ways, and he held my hair. His touch
was soft. He touched me. I barely felt him. He made the music sound
different, melodies changed, songs vanished. Perhaps it feared him,
the air. It moved so differently around him. I clutched the cross, the
man who hung from it, his dying body, and the devil held my breast.
I felt the warmth and wondered where it came from. (Bowie, you sound
so different). I breathed and he breathed. I moved and he moved.
He vanished, and I longed for him. He returned, and I feared him.
I feared him. I feared him.
'Lay me down,' I said. He lay me down.
'In the field.' He took me there.
'Where I am everything.' And I was.
'Where I am nothing.' And I was.

Rosina Benton

The River Has An Eye

The river has an eye
it knows who drowned the little girl
daughter of a fisherman,
(who too smelt of fish)
whose breast sunk like a stone
beneath the river's golden flesh
into its swollen heart

The river has an arm,
it grabbed her little ankle
with a fist of silver mud
and took her little anklet
made of blood and bone
and beneath the river's silver flesh
gathered in its ever-swollen heart

The river has a voice
of silver and of gold
when on a broken-hearted night
her tears fell into the river
into its satin flesh,
then the river sang his song
'Drink the sky my beauty
the moon is at your lips'
(and her tears were waiting
in his very swollen heart)

Brook Benton

Falling Like Bleeding

dangling on a slipknot of desire.
not even the mercy
of hitting rock bottom,
eating alice cookies.

feeding an addiction
to anticipation.
and when the punch comes
i take it like a blast in the ahhhhrrm.

stumbling is the cripple's way,
and as i take out the sand paper
to remind myself, sylvia and the moon
watch on with their o-gape of despair.

unseen danger don't scare me.
courting death and the rapist
on a nightly basis
as i smear my scent, like a cat
around the unlocked doors and windows.

falling like bleeding

falling like bleeding

falling like bleeding.

Kerryn Tredrea

Outlines

And don't you find that barbed wire
will remind you of shaven heads
torn bodies
knotted limbs
hands of bones?

Or those old black and white newsreels
you see with the drumming of guns
dead men running
to be blown away
in crumpled smoke?

The fence along this road has snared
on its barbs some wisps of paper
a clutch of hair
snatch of blue cloth
the carcass of a crow.

In the mountains of Mexico I have known
lines formed from barbed wire
with garments like
snappy kits pegged
between each spur

and little girls with laughing skirts,
braided hair, were counting out their clothes.

Elaine Barker

Fishing

his mit-like hands
finger the delicate line
pulling circles
within circles

his narrowed eyes
focus on the lure
study the arrangement
of tackle

at the edge of the pond
he arches back
then leans the rod
towards the water

with a flick
he tips the surface
pulls back and up
and back

dog races around the pond
the horse clambers up the hill
even a duck has skidded in
to watch proceedings

I wade through wet clay
then glide
across the straps of weed
into the depths

I float to where
the warmth of the water
turns . . .
a mild panic

suspended in the cool black
I watch him cast spells
from the edge
lassoing his dreams.

H A Sladdin

Evensong

When I die
I will go with the plovers
You'll hear my solitary call near the creek
as the cloud clears the moon
I'll pass over.

I'll watch between blades of grass for hours
my world of shiny eyes in small dark holds
beetles in ditches
grubs on thistle stalks
while a neighbouring heron
concentrates in the reeds.

I'll never leave the earth
only dip my wings over it,
looking,
where there are people
I'll turn away quickly
my shadow long in the evening sun.

Margaret Reichardt

Death With Seahorse

A few days before her death
she showed me a sea horse
penny-sized, in her palm.

In the casual way of the beach
we were first names, weather
a hail from the sea
where she swam year round,
tanned shoulders a sheen
on the breaker line.

The white maelstrom of winter surf
snapped her neck like shortbread,
dumped her, a discarded toy.
Just two days later they switched off
the maze of tubes and monitors
crowding her white bed.

I learned she was dead only by chance,
buried a few days before,
leaving me the memory of a sea horse
curled up in her hand,
like an embryo.

David Cookson

For further information about
Friendly Street publications and activities please visit
www.friendlystreetpoets.org.au

§